MW01439440

Leader
to be

Adam Green

Responsible Choices, Resilient Leaders: Navigating Campus Life with Integrity

Table Of Contents

Chapter 1: Introduction to Responsible Choices and Resilient Leadership	5
Understanding the Importance of Responsible Choices on Campus	5
The Role of Resilient Leadership in Campus Life	6
Chapter 2: Developing Effective Study Habits for Academic Success	8
Setting Clear Goals and Priorities	8
Creating a Productive Study Environment	10
Time Management Techniques for Efficient Studying	12
Effective Note-Taking Strategies	14
Utilizing Resources and Seeking Help	16
Chapter 3: Time Management: Maximizing Productivity and Balance	17
Understanding the Value of Time	17
Setting Realistic Goals and Deadlines	19
Strategies for Prioritizing Tasks	20
Overcoming Procrastination	22
Balancing Academics, Extracurriculars, and Personal Life	24

(c) 2024: Responsible Choices, Resilient Leaders: Navigating Campus Life with Integrity

Responsible Choices, Resilient Leaders: Navigating Campus Life with Integrity

Chapter 4: Leadership Skills: Inspiring and Motivating Others	**25**
Identifying and Developing Leadership Qualities	25
Effective Communication for Leadership	27
Building Trust and Confidence in Your Leadership	29
Conflict Resolution and Decision-Making	30
Empowering and Supporting Others	32
Chapter 5: Sobriety: Making Healthy Choices in a Campus Environment	**34**
Understanding the Risks and Consequences of Substance Abuse	34
Developing Personal Strategies for Sobriety	36
Navigating Peer Pressure and Social Situations	37
Finding Support and Resources for Recovery	39
Promoting a Culture of Responsibility and Sobriety on Campus	40
Chapter 6: Morality and Ethics: Making Ethical Decisions in Campus Life	**42**
Understanding Personal Values and Beliefs	42
Ethical Dilemmas on Campus and How to Navigate Them	44

(c) 2024: Responsible Choices, Resilient Leaders: Navigating Campus Life with Integrity

Responsible Choices, Resilient Leaders: Navigating Campus Life with Integrity

Developing a Moral Compass for Decision-Making	45
Promoting Integrity and Honesty in Campus Interactions	47
Fostering a Culture of Ethical Behavior and Accountability	48
Chapter 7: Building Healthy Relationships: Nurturing Connections on Campus	50
Understanding the Importance of Healthy Relationships	50
Communication Skills for Building Strong Connections	52
Developing Empathy and Emotional Intelligence	53
Resolving Conflict and Building Trust	55
Creating a Supportive and Inclusive Community	57
Chapter 8: Responsible Choices: Making Sound Decisions in Campus Life	58
Assessing the Consequences of Choices and Actions	58
Recognizing Peer Influence and Making Independent Decisions	60
Seeking Guidance and Mentorship for Decision-Making	62
Resisting Negative Influences and Temptations	63
Cultivating a Culture of Responsibility and Accountability on Campus	65

(c) 2024: Responsible Choices, Resilient Leaders: Navigating Campus Life with Integrity

Responsible Choices, Resilient Leaders: Navigating Campus Life with Integrity

Chapter 9: Nurturing a Relationship with God: Spirituality on Campus — 66

    Exploring the Role of Spirituality in Leadership — 66

    Finding Meaning and Purpose in Campus Life — 68

    Practicing Mindfulness and Self-Reflection — 70

    Engaging in Spiritual Practices and Rituals — 71

    Connecting with Faith-Based Communities on Campus — 71

Chapter 10: Conclusion: Embracing Responsible Choices and Resilient Leadership — **72**

    Reflecting on Personal Growth and Development — 72

    Setting Long-Term Goals for Continued Leadership — 72

    Embracing a Lifelong Commitment to Responsible Choices — 72

    Inspiring and Influencing Others to Navigate Campus Life with Integrity — 72

    Celebrating the Journey of Responsible Choices and Resilient Leadership — 72

Responsible Choices, Resilient Leaders: Navigating Campus Life with Integrity

Chapter 1: Introduction to Responsible Choices and Resilient Leadership

Understanding the Importance of Responsible Choices on Campus

Aspiring leaders on campus play a vital role in shaping the environment and culture of their educational institutions. To achieve success in this endeavor, it is imperative that they understand the importance of making responsible choices. In the book "Responsible Choices, Resilient Leaders: Navigating Campus Life with Integrity," we explore the significance of responsible decision-making in various aspects of campus life, including study habits, time management, leadership, sobriety, morality, healthy relationships, responsible choices, and a serious relationship with God.

One of the key areas where responsible choices are crucial is in the realm of study habits. Aspiring leaders must recognize the value of prioritizing their academic commitments and developing effective study strategies. By dedicating ample time to their studies, setting realistic goals, and seeking academic support when needed, these leaders can establish a strong foundation for their future success.

Time management is another vital aspect that aspiring leaders must master. Balancing multiple responsibilities and commitments requires effective organization and prioritization. By managing their time wisely, leaders can ensure productivity in all areas of their campus involvement, while also maintaining a healthy work-life balance.

Leadership is a core trait that aspiring leaders need to cultivate. Responsible choices in leadership involve leading by example, demonstrating integrity, and promoting inclusivity and empathy. By fostering a positive and ethical leadership style, these individuals can inspire others to follow suit and make responsible choices themselves.

Responsible Choices, Resilient Leaders: Navigating Campus Life with Integrity

Sobriety and morality are essential values that aspiring leaders must uphold. Responsible choices in this regard involve abstaining from substance abuse, respecting oneself and others, and adhering to a strong moral compass. By maintaining sobriety and practicing morality, leaders can create a safe and nurturing environment for their peers.

Healthy relationships are crucial in the development of aspiring leaders. Responsible choices in relationships involve fostering positive connections, promoting communication and respect, and avoiding harmful behaviors. By cultivating healthy relationships, leaders can build a strong support system and ensure their personal growth and success.

Lastly, a serious relationship with God can provide aspiring leaders with a solid spiritual foundation. Responsible choices in this realm involve seeking guidance, practicing faith-based values, and staying connected to one's beliefs. By nurturing a relationship with God, leaders can find strength, purpose, and guidance in their journey.

In conclusion, understanding the importance of responsible choices on campus is fundamental for aspiring leaders. By prioritizing effective study habits, time management, leadership, sobriety, morality, healthy relationships, responsible choices, and a serious relationship with God, these leaders can navigate campus life with integrity and achieve success in their endeavors. This subchapter serves as a comprehensive guide for aspiring leaders, empowering them to make responsible choices and become resilient leaders in their campus communities.

The Role of Resilient Leadership in Campus Life

Responsible Choices, Resilient Leaders: Navigating Campus Life with Integrity

In the fast-paced and challenging environment of campus life, aspiring leaders must develop resilience to navigate the complexities and demands they face. Resilient leadership plays a crucial role in achieving success through effective study habits, time management, leadership, sobriety, morality, healthy relationships, responsible choices, and a serious relationship with God. In this subchapter, we will explore the significance of resilient leadership and how it can positively impact your campus experience.

Resilient leadership begins with a strong foundation of self-discipline and determination. As an aspiring leader, you must cultivate effective study habits to excel academically. By adopting strategies such as prioritizing tasks, setting realistic goals, and managing your time efficiently, you can develop the resilience needed to overcome academic challenges and achieve success.

Furthermore, resilient leaders understand the importance of balancing their commitments and responsibilities. Effective time management skills enable you to juggle various activities without compromising your performance. By establishing a schedule and learning to prioritize tasks, you can optimize your productivity, reduce stress, and make the most of your campus experience.

Leadership is not limited to formal positions; it can be demonstrated in various aspects of campus life. Resilient leaders actively engage in clubs, organizations, and community service, seeking opportunities to make a positive impact. By taking on leadership roles and responsibilities, you can develop essential skills such as teamwork, communication, and problem-solving, which are invaluable in both your personal and professional life.

Resilient leadership also entails making responsible choices and maintaining sobriety. By abstaining from harmful substances and making wise decisions, you can protect your physical and mental well-being. Additionally, resilient leaders prioritize morality and uphold ethical standards, serving as role models for others.

Healthy relationships are crucial in campus life, and resilient leaders strive to build and maintain them. By fostering meaningful connections with peers, professors, and mentors, you create a support system that can help you navigate challenges and celebrate achievements. These relationships contribute to personal growth, emotional well-being, and overall success.

Finally, a serious relationship with God can provide a strong foundation for resilient leadership. By cultivating spiritual practices, such as prayer, meditation, and reflection, you can find guidance, strength, and resilience in your faith. This relationship can serve as a source of inspiration, wisdom, and comfort throughout your campus journey.

In conclusion, resilient leadership is essential for aspiring leaders seeking success in various aspects of campus life. By developing effective study habits, time management skills, leadership qualities, sobriety, morality, healthy relationships, responsible choices, and a serious relationship with God, you can navigate the challenges of campus life with integrity. Embrace the role of resilient leadership and empower yourself to make a positive impact on your campus community and beyond.

Chapter 2: Developing Effective Study Habits for Academic Success

Setting Clear Goals and Priorities

Responsible Choices, Resilient Leaders: Navigating Campus Life with Integrity

Aspiring leaders, whether on campus or in any other aspect of life, understand the importance of setting clear goals and priorities. This subchapter will explore the significance of this practice and provide practical tips on how to effectively set goals and establish priorities to achieve success in various areas of your life.

Goal setting is a crucial skill for any leader. It allows you to envision your desired outcome and work towards it with purpose and determination. When setting goals, it is important to make them specific, measurable, achievable, relevant, and time-bound (SMART). By following this framework, you can ensure that your goals are realistic and attainable, keeping you motivated and focused.

Prioritizing is another essential aspect of effective leadership. As a student leader, you may find yourself juggling multiple responsibilities and commitments. By establishing priorities, you can allocate your time and energy efficiently, ensuring that you make progress in all areas that matter to you.

To set clear goals and establish priorities, start by defining your values and long-term vision. Understand what truly matters to you and what you want to achieve in your time as a leader on campus. This will provide you with a solid foundation upon which to build your goals and priorities.

Break down your long-term vision into smaller, actionable goals. These should be specific and aligned with your values. For example, if you value academic success, a goal could be to maintain a certain GPA or graduate with honors. Prioritize these goals based on their importance and urgency. This will help you focus on what matters most and prevent you from feeling overwhelmed.

To effectively manage your time and resources, consider using tools like a planner or a digital calendar. These can help you map out your commitments, deadlines, and important events. Additionally, learn to say no to non-essential tasks or commitments that do not align with your goals and priorities. This will allow you to maintain focus on what truly matters and avoid unnecessary distractions.

Remember that setting clear goals and establishing priorities is not a one-time task. It requires regular evaluation and adjustment. Take time to reflect on your progress, celebrate your achievements, and make necessary changes to stay on track.

By setting clear goals and establishing priorities, you can become a resilient leader who effectively navigates campus life with integrity. This practice will empower you to develop effective study habits, manage your time wisely, make responsible choices, maintain healthy relationships, and cultivate a serious relationship with God. Embrace this skill, and you will be well on your way to achieving success and making a positive impact as a leader on campus.

Creating a Productive Study Environment

As aspiring leaders, it is crucial to understand the importance of creating a productive study environment. The way you approach your studies not only impacts your academic success but also lays the foundation for your overall growth as a leader. In this subchapter, we will explore effective strategies to help you cultivate a study environment that fosters focus, productivity, and personal development.

1. Find your ideal study space: Identify a location where you can concentrate without distractions. This could be a quiet corner in the library, a dedicated study room, or even your own room if it offers a conducive atmosphere. Experiment with different environments until you discover the one that works best for you.

Responsible Choices, Resilient Leaders: Navigating Campus Life with Integrity

2. Eliminate distractions: Minimize interruptions and distractions by turning off notifications on your phone or computer. Consider using website blockers or apps that limit access to social media during study sessions. Create a physical space that is free from clutter, allowing you to focus solely on your work.

3. Establish a study routine: Develop a consistent study schedule that aligns with your natural energy levels and commitments. Set specific time blocks for studying and stick to them. By creating a routine, you train your mind to be in the study mode during those designated periods, leading to increased productivity.

4. Utilize effective time management techniques: Employ time management strategies such as the Pomodoro Technique, where you work for focused intervals followed by short breaks. Prioritize tasks using tools like to-do lists or calendars. By effectively managing your time, you can ensure that you allocate sufficient hours for studying while balancing other responsibilities.

5. Optimize your study materials: Organize your study materials in a way that facilitates efficient learning. Use color-coded notes, highlighters, and flashcards to aid memory retention. Consider utilizing online resources, such as digital textbooks or educational apps, to enhance your understanding of the subject matter.

6. Collaborate and seek support: Engage in group study sessions or form study groups with like-minded individuals. Collaborating with peers can provide new perspectives and enhance comprehension. Additionally, seeking support from mentors, professors, or academic resources can strengthen your knowledge base and boost your academic performance.

Remember, a productive study environment is not solely limited to physical aspects but also encompasses mental and emotional well-being. Practice self-care by getting enough rest, exercising regularly, and maintaining a healthy diet. Prioritize your mental health by taking breaks when needed and seeking support when feeling overwhelmed.

By creating a productive study environment, you set yourself up for success in all areas of life. As an aspiring leader, your commitment to effective study habits and responsible choices will not only enhance your academic journey but also shape you into a resilient and influential leader on campus. Embrace these strategies and unlock your full potential as you navigate campus life with integrity.

Time Management Techniques for Efficient Studying

Time management is a crucial skill for aspiring leaders who want to achieve success in their academic pursuits and develop effective study habits. In this subchapter, we will explore various time management techniques that can help you maximize your productivity and make the most out of your study sessions.

1. Prioritize and plan: Begin by identifying your most important tasks and create a study schedule that aligns with your goals. Allocate dedicated time slots for each subject or topic, ensuring that you give more attention to challenging subjects while leaving time for breaks and leisure activities to maintain a healthy balance.

2. Set realistic goals: Break down your study goals into smaller, manageable tasks. This approach not only makes your goals more attainable but also provides a sense of accomplishment as you complete each task. Additionally, setting specific deadlines for each task can help you stay motivated and on track.

3. Eliminate distractions: Create an environment conducive to focused studying. Minimize distractions by turning off your phone or putting it on silent mode, closing unnecessary tabs on your computer, and finding a quiet place where you can concentrate. Consider using website blockers or productivity apps to limit your access to social media during study sessions.

4. Implement the Pomodoro Technique: This time management technique involves working in short, focused bursts followed by short breaks. Set a timer for 25 minutes of uninterrupted studying, then take a 5-minute break. After completing four Pomodoro cycles, reward yourself with a longer break. This method can help increase concentration and prevent burnout.

5. Use effective study techniques: Experiment with different study techniques and find what works best for you. Some popular methods include active reading, summarizing information in your own words, creating flashcards, and teaching concepts to others. By finding the most effective study techniques, you can optimize your learning and retention.

6. Practice self-care: Taking care of your physical and mental well-being is essential for efficient studying. Get enough sleep, eat nutritious meals, and engage in regular exercise to maintain optimal energy levels. Additionally, take breaks during long study sessions to relax and recharge.

By incorporating these time management techniques into your study routine, you can enhance your productivity, achieve academic success, and develop the necessary skills to become a resilient and effective leader on campus. Remember that responsible choices, including maintaining sobriety, practicing morality, building healthy relationships, and nurturing a serious relationship with God, are integral components of a well-rounded and successful leadership journey.

Effective Note-Taking Strategies

In the journey of becoming a leader on campus and achieving success, one crucial skill that aspiring leaders must develop is effective note-taking. Taking effective notes not only helps you retain and recall information better but also allows you to organize your thoughts and ideas, leading to more productive study sessions and improved academic performance. In this subchapter, we will explore some tried-and-true note-taking strategies that will set you on the path to success.

1. Active Listening: Effective note-taking starts with active listening. Pay close attention to the speaker or lecturer, focusing on key points, examples, and supporting details. Use abbreviations and symbols to capture information quickly and efficiently.

2. Choose the Right Format: Different individuals have different preferences when it comes to note-taking formats. Find a format that works best for you, whether it's the traditional outline method, flowcharts, mind maps, or a combination of these. Experiment with different formats until you find what suits your learning style and helps you understand and remember the material.

Responsible Choices, Resilient Leaders: Navigating Campus Life with Integrity

3. Be Selective: It's impossible to write down every single word that is said during a lecture or presentation. Instead, focus on capturing the main ideas and supporting details. Listen for cues from the speaker, such as repeated phrases or emphasized points, to identify what's most important.

4. Organization is Key: Organize your notes in a logical and structured manner. Use headings, subheadings, and bullet points to create a clear hierarchy of information. This will make it easier to review and study your notes later.

5. Review and Revise: Regularly review your notes to reinforce your understanding of the material. Take the time to fill in any missing information, clarify confusing points, and make connections between different ideas. The act of reviewing and revising your notes shortly after the lecture will help solidify the information in your memory.

6. Use Visuals: Incorporate visual aids, such as diagrams, graphs, or illustrations, into your notes whenever possible. Visuals can help you better comprehend complex concepts and make connections between different ideas.

Remember, effective note-taking is not just about capturing information; it's about actively engaging with the material and making it your own. By implementing these strategies, you will not only enhance your academic performance but also develop vital skills that will serve you well in your leadership journey. So, grab your notebook and pen, and start taking notes like a true leader!

*Note: This subchapter on effective note-taking is part of the book "Responsible Choices, Resilient Leaders: Navigating Campus Life with Integrity" aimed at aspiring leaders who seek success through effective study habits, time management, leadership, sobriety, morality, healthy relationships, responsible choices, and a serious relationship with God.

(c) 2024: Responsible Choices, Resilient Leaders: Navigating Campus Life with Integrity

Utilizing Resources and Seeking Help

In the journey of becoming an aspiring leader on campus, it is essential to recognize that no one can achieve success entirely on their own. To truly excel and make a positive impact, it is crucial to utilize the resources available to you and seek help when needed. This subchapter aims to guide you through this process, emphasizing the importance of effective study habits, time management, leadership, sobriety, morality, healthy relationships, responsible choices, and a serious relationship with God.

One of the first steps towards utilizing resources effectively is understanding your unique strengths and weaknesses. Take the time to reflect on your areas of expertise, as well as areas that require improvement. By acknowledging your weaknesses, you can seek out appropriate resources, such as tutoring services, study groups, or time management workshops, to help you overcome obstacles and grow as a leader.

Time management is another critical aspect to consider. As an aspiring leader, your schedule will likely be filled with various commitments and responsibilities. Learning to prioritize tasks, set realistic goals, and manage your time efficiently will not only enhance your productivity but also provide you with more opportunities to engage in other aspects of your life. Utilize calendars, planner apps, or time-blocking techniques to ensure you stay organized and make the most of your time.

Leadership is not just about personal growth; it also involves supporting and empowering others. Recognize that seeking help is not a sign of weakness but rather demonstrates your commitment to personal and collective growth. Build a network of mentors, advisors, and peers who can provide guidance, support, and valuable insights. Engage in leadership development programs, attend workshops, and take advantage of campus resources dedicated to personal and professional growth.

Furthermore, maintaining sobriety, practicing morality, and fostering healthy relationships are all integral components of responsible leadership. Surround yourself with individuals who share your values and encourage your personal growth. Seek support from campus organizations that promote healthy lifestyles, provide counseling services, or offer peer support.

Lastly, nurturing a serious relationship with God can provide a strong foundation for your leadership journey. Take time for self-reflection, meditation, and prayer to cultivate a sense of purpose, guidance, and spiritual well-being. Engage in faith-based campus organizations, attend religious services, and seek out spiritual mentors who can support and guide your spiritual growth.

In conclusion, as an aspiring leader, it is essential to utilize the resources and seek help available to you. By developing effective study habits, practicing time management, prioritizing leadership, maintaining sobriety and morality, fostering healthy relationships, making responsible choices, and nurturing a serious relationship with God, you will not only excel in your personal and academic endeavors but also become a resilient leader who positively impacts your campus community. Remember, great leaders are not afraid to ask for help and utilize the resources at their disposal.

Chapter 3: Time Management: Maximizing Productivity and Balance

Understanding the Value of Time

Responsible Choices, Resilient Leaders: Navigating Campus Life with Integrity

As aspiring leaders, it is crucial to understand the value of time and how it can impact our success in various aspects of life. Time is a limited resource that cannot be replenished, making it one of the most valuable assets we possess. In this subchapter, we will explore the significance of time management and its role in achieving success on campus, maintaining healthy relationships, making responsible choices, and nurturing our relationship with God.

Effective time management is a cornerstone of leadership and is essential for achieving success in any endeavor. It involves setting priorities, creating schedules, and adhering to deadlines. By managing our time wisely, we can allocate sufficient hours for studying, engaging in extracurricular activities, and pursuing personal interests. This not only enhances our academic performance but also allows us to develop essential skills such as discipline, organization, and resilience.

Moreover, understanding the value of time helps us cultivate healthy relationships. Time is a precious gift we can offer to our friends, family, and loved ones. By prioritizing quality time with others, we strengthen our bonds and create lasting connections. Actively listening, being present, and showing genuine interest in others' lives demonstrate respect and care, fostering meaningful relationships.

Responsible choices are also deeply influenced by our understanding of time's value. When we comprehend that time is not limitless, we become more mindful of the consequences of our actions. We are more likely to make choices that align with our values, prioritize our goals, and contribute positively to our communities. This understanding empowers us to resist peer pressure, make ethical decisions, and lead by example.

Lastly, our relationship with God can be nurtured through a sincere appreciation for the value of time. Allocating dedicated time for prayer, reflection, and spiritual growth allows us to deepen our faith and find guidance in our leadership journey. By recognizing that time spent with God is an investment in our spiritual well-being, we can develop a stronger connection to our beliefs and gain the strength and wisdom to lead with integrity.

In conclusion, understanding the value of time is fundamental for aspiring leaders on campus. Effective time management empowers us to excel academically, build healthy relationships, make responsible choices, and strengthen our relationship with God. By embracing the importance of time, we can maximize our potential, make a positive impact, and navigate campus life with integrity.

Setting Realistic Goals and Deadlines

As an aspiring leader, one of the most crucial skills you can cultivate is the ability to set realistic goals and deadlines. In order to achieve success on campus, it is essential to develop effective study habits, manage your time efficiently, and make responsible choices. This subchapter will guide you through the process of setting goals and deadlines that align with your values and priorities, while also fostering a serious relationship with God.

To begin, it is important to understand that setting realistic goals requires self-awareness and introspection. Take the time to reflect on your strengths, weaknesses, and passions. What are your long-term aspirations? What steps can you take to achieve them while remaining true to your values? By asking yourself these questions, you can create a framework that will guide you in setting achievable goals.

Responsible Choices, Resilient Leaders: Navigating Campus Life with Integrity

Once you have identified your goals, it is crucial to establish deadlines for each of them. Deadlines provide structure and help to keep you accountable. However, it is important to set deadlines that are realistic and attainable. Pushing yourself too hard can lead to burnout and diminish the quality of your work. Break down your goals into smaller, manageable tasks, and assign deadlines to each of them. This will ensure that you stay on track and make progress towards your ultimate objectives.

Effective time management is another key component of setting realistic goals and deadlines. Prioritize your tasks and allocate sufficient time to each of them. Avoid procrastination by creating a schedule and sticking to it. Additionally, ensure that you allow for breaks and self-care activities in your routine. Taking care of your physical and mental well-being is essential for maintaining productivity and focus.

Lastly, remember to cultivate a serious relationship with God throughout this process. Seek guidance and wisdom through prayer and meditation. Allow your faith to influence your decision-making and keep you grounded. By aligning your goals and deadlines with your spiritual beliefs, you will not only achieve success but also maintain a sense of purpose and integrity.

In conclusion, setting realistic goals and deadlines is a fundamental aspect of becoming a resilient leader on campus. By developing effective study habits, managing your time efficiently, making responsible choices, and nurturing a serious relationship with God, you can achieve success while remaining true to your values. Embrace self-awareness, prioritize your tasks, and allocate sufficient time to each of them. Remember to stay focused, take breaks, and seek guidance from your faith. With these principles in mind, you can navigate campus life with integrity and become a responsible and resilient leader.

Strategies for Prioritizing Tasks

Responsible Choices, Resilient Leaders: Navigating Campus Life with Integrity

As an aspiring leader on campus, effective time management and prioritization of tasks are key skills that will help you achieve success in all aspects of your academic and personal life. In this subchapter, we will explore strategies that will enable you to stay organized, make responsible choices, and navigate campus life with integrity.

1. Create a To-Do List: Start by listing down all the tasks you need to accomplish, whether it's assignments, studying, attending meetings, or personal commitments. Break down larger tasks into smaller, more manageable subtasks. By having a clear visual representation of your responsibilities, you can prioritize them based on deadlines and importance.

2. Identify Urgent vs. Important: Differentiate between urgent tasks that require immediate attention and important tasks that contribute to your long-term goals. Urgent tasks may be time-sensitive, but important tasks may have a greater impact on your overall success. Focus on completing tasks that are both urgent and important first, and then move on to those that are important but not necessarily urgent.

3. Utilize Time Blocking: Allocate specific time blocks for different activities on your schedule. This technique helps you avoid multitasking and ensures that you dedicate focused time to each task. For example, set aside dedicated study hours, time for extracurricular activities, and personal relaxation time. This way, you can avoid feeling overwhelmed and maintain a healthy work-life balance.

4. Learn to Delegate: As a leader, it's crucial to recognize when you can't handle everything on your plate. Delegate tasks to capable individuals who can assist you in accomplishing your goals. This not only helps lighten your load but also fosters collaboration and teamwork, which are essential qualities of a successful leader.

5. Practice the 80/20 Rule: The Pareto Principle states that 80% of your results come from 20% of your efforts. Identify the tasks that will yield the most significant outcomes and prioritize them accordingly. By focusing on the most impactful tasks, you can maximize your productivity and achieve your goals more efficiently.

6. Learn to Say No: As an aspiring leader, it's important to recognize your limits and set boundaries. Avoid overcommitting yourself by saying no to tasks or activities that don't align with your goals or values. By doing so, you can prioritize your time and energy on tasks that truly matter.

Remember, effective task prioritization is not just about completing tasks; it's about making responsible choices that align with your values, maintain your integrity, and contribute to your overall success. By implementing these strategies, you will not only become a more efficient leader but also develop strong study habits, time management skills, and a healthy work-life balance. Embrace these strategies, stay focused, and always strive for excellence as you navigate campus life with integrity.

Overcoming Procrastination

Procrastination is a common challenge that many aspiring leaders face on their journey towards success. It is the art of delaying or postponing tasks that need to be done, often resulting in unnecessary stress, missed opportunities, and compromised effectiveness. However, by adopting a proactive approach and implementing effective strategies, you can overcome procrastination and unlock your true potential as a leader.

Responsible Choices, Resilient Leaders: Navigating Campus Life with Integrity

One of the key factors in overcoming procrastination is developing effective study habits. As an aspiring leader, academic excellence is crucial, and this requires discipline and consistency in your approach to studying. Create a study schedule that aligns with your personal preferences and learning style. Set specific goals for each study session and break down larger tasks into smaller, manageable ones. This will help you stay focused and motivated, ultimately enhancing your productivity.

Time management plays a vital role in combating procrastination. Leaders understand the value of time and the importance of prioritizing tasks. Learn to identify and eliminate time-wasting activities, such as excessive social media usage or idle conversations. Utilize tools like calendars, to-do lists, and reminders to stay organized and stay on track. By effectively managing your time, you can allocate sufficient hours to both your academic commitments and extracurricular activities, ensuring a well-balanced and successful campus life.

Leadership is not just about academic achievements; it also encompasses qualities such as sobriety, morality, and healthy relationships. Procrastination can hinder your ability to develop these essential attributes. By overcoming procrastination, you can create space for personal growth and self-reflection, allowing you to make responsible choices that align with your values. Embrace the challenge of overcoming procrastination and use it as an opportunity to strengthen your character and deepen your relationship with God.

To overcome procrastination, start by setting realistic goals and deadlines for yourself. Break larger tasks into smaller, more manageable ones, and tackle them one at a time. Hold yourself accountable by seeking support from your peers or joining study groups that encourage productivity. Surround yourself with like-minded individuals who share your drive and ambition, as they can serve as a source of motivation and inspiration.

(c) 2024: Responsible Choices, Resilient Leaders: Navigating Campus Life with Integrity

Remember, overcoming procrastination is not a one-time achievement but an ongoing process. It requires self-discipline, determination, and a commitment to personal growth. As an aspiring leader, embrace the opportunity to overcome procrastination and unlock your true potential. By developing effective study habits, practicing time management, making responsible choices, and nurturing a serious relationship with God, you will not only overcome procrastination but also cultivate the qualities necessary to become a resilient and successful leader on campus.

Balancing Academics, Extracurriculars, and Personal Life

As an aspiring leader on campus, you undoubtedly have a multitude of responsibilities pulling you in different directions. From excelling in your academic pursuits to actively engaging in extracurricular activities and maintaining a healthy personal life, finding the perfect equilibrium can seem like an impossible task. However, with effective study habits, time management skills, and a focus on making responsible choices, you can navigate the complexities of campus life with integrity and achieve success.

The first step towards balancing academics, extracurriculars, and personal life is to establish effective study habits. Set specific goals for each study session and create a schedule that allows for dedicated time to focus on your coursework. Avoid procrastination by breaking larger tasks into smaller, manageable ones. Prioritize your assignments and tackle them one by one, ensuring that you allocate enough time for each task. Utilize effective study techniques such as active reading, note-taking, and creating study groups to enhance your learning experience.

Responsible Choices, Resilient Leaders: Navigating Campus Life with Integrity

Time management is crucial when it comes to juggling numerous responsibilities. Learn to prioritize your commitments and allocate time accordingly. Create a daily or weekly planner to keep track of deadlines, meetings, and personal obligations. Be realistic about how much you can handle and learn to say no when necessary. Remember, it's better to excel in a few areas rather than spreading yourself too thin.

Leadership, sobriety, morality, healthy relationships, and responsible choices are all integral to your personal and professional growth. Surround yourself with like-minded individuals who share your values and aspirations. Seek out mentorship opportunities and engage in activities that align with your personal beliefs. Strive to be a positive influence on those around you and make responsible choices that reflect your integrity and character.

Finally, maintaining a serious relationship with God can provide the foundation for your journey as a leader. Nurture your spiritual well-being through regular prayer, meditation, and reflection. Seek guidance from your faith community and use your beliefs to guide your actions and decision-making processes.

Balancing academics, extracurriculars, and personal life may require some trial and error, but with perseverance and a commitment to self-improvement, you can achieve success. Remember to prioritize self-care, take breaks when needed, and seek support from friends, family, and campus resources. By cultivating effective study habits, managing your time wisely, making responsible choices, and staying true to your values, you can navigate campus life with integrity and become a resilient leader.

Chapter 4: Leadership Skills: Inspiring and Motivating Others

Identifying and Developing Leadership Qualities

Responsible Choices, Resilient Leaders: Navigating Campus Life with Integrity

Leadership is not just a title; it is a mindset and a set of skills that can be developed and honed over time. In this subchapter, we will explore the key qualities that aspiring leaders should possess and how they can cultivate these qualities to navigate campus life successfully with integrity. Whether you are a student leader, a club president, or simply someone who wants to make a positive impact, this chapter will provide you with actionable insights to develop your leadership potential.

First and foremost, self-awareness is crucial for effective leadership. Understanding your strengths and weaknesses allows you to leverage your skills and seek opportunities for growth. Take the time to reflect on your values, personality traits, and areas where you excel. This self-reflection will help you align your actions with your values and make responsible choices that reflect integrity.

A leader must also be able to communicate effectively. This involves not only expressing your thoughts clearly but also active listening and empathy. By developing strong communication skills, you can build healthy relationships with your peers, mentors, and teammates. Effective communication also allows you to delegate tasks, resolve conflicts, and motivate others towards a common goal.

Time management is another crucial aspect of leadership. Aspiring leaders must learn to prioritize tasks, set goals, and manage their time efficiently. By mastering effective study habits and time management techniques, you can achieve academic success while still devoting time to leadership responsibilities.

In addition to these qualities, maintaining sobriety and making responsible choices are essential for a leader's credibility. Avoiding substance abuse and making ethical decisions will not only preserve your reputation but also inspire others to follow your lead. A leader should exhibit strong moral values and act as a role model for their peers.

(c) 2024: Responsible Choices, Resilient Leaders: Navigating Campus Life with Integrity

Lastly, a serious relationship with God can provide the foundation for a leader's actions and decisions. Cultivating spirituality helps leaders connect with their inner selves, find purpose, and seek guidance when faced with difficult choices. By nurturing this relationship, aspiring leaders can find strength and inspiration to navigate campus life with integrity.

In conclusion, identifying and developing leadership qualities is crucial for aspiring leaders who aim to make a positive impact on campus. By fostering self-awareness, effective communication, time management skills, sobriety, morality, responsible choices, and a deep relationship with God, individuals can cultivate the qualities necessary for successful leadership. Embracing these qualities will not only enhance your personal growth but also make you a respected and influential leader in your community.

Effective Communication for Leadership

In the journey towards becoming a successful leader on campus, one of the most crucial skills to develop is effective communication. As aspiring leaders, it is essential to recognize that effective communication is the foundation upon which all other leadership qualities are built. Whether it is conveying your vision, motivating others, or resolving conflicts, mastering the art of communication is what sets exceptional leaders apart from the rest.

Good leaders understand that communication is a two-way street. It involves not only speaking clearly and articulately but also actively listening to others. By actively listening, leaders can gain valuable insights, understand different perspectives, and build stronger relationships. This skill is especially important when working with diverse groups of individuals who may have varying opinions and experiences.

Responsible Choices, Resilient Leaders: Navigating Campus Life with Integrity

Another aspect of effective communication is non-verbal cues. As leaders, we must be mindful of our body language, facial expressions, and gestures, as they can convey messages even more strongly than words. Maintaining eye contact, showing empathy through nodding or affirming gestures, and using open and inviting body language can greatly enhance the impact of our communication.

Furthermore, effective communication involves choosing the right medium for conveying your message. In today's digital age, leaders must be adept at utilizing various communication platforms, such as email, social media, and video conferencing. However, it is essential to remember that face-to-face communication is often the most powerful and authentic way to connect with others. Taking the time to have personal conversations can foster trust, build rapport, and create lasting bonds.

Leaders who prioritize effective communication also understand the importance of clarity in their messages. They avoid jargon, use simple language, and ensure that their ideas are easily understood by everyone. It is crucial to tailor your communication style to the audience you are addressing, ensuring that you are relatable and engaging.

Lastly, effective communication is not just about transmitting information but also about inspiring and motivating others. Leaders who can convey their passion, vision, and values with enthusiasm and conviction can inspire and mobilize their teams to achieve great things.

(c) 2024: Responsible Choices, Resilient Leaders: Navigating Campus Life with Integrity

In conclusion, effective communication is an essential skill for aspiring leaders. By actively listening, utilizing non-verbal cues, choosing the right medium, maintaining clarity, and inspiring others, leaders can effectively convey their messages, build stronger relationships, and achieve success in their various roles. Developing and honing these communication skills will not only benefit leaders in their campus endeavors but also in their personal and professional lives. Remember, communication is the key to unlocking the potential within yourself and those around you.

Building Trust and Confidence in Your Leadership

As an aspiring leader on campus, it is crucial to understand the importance of building trust and confidence among your peers and followers. Trust is the foundation upon which successful leadership is built, and without it, your ability to lead effectively will be severely compromised. In this subchapter, we will explore key strategies and principles that will help you establish and maintain trust and confidence in your leadership journey.

One of the fundamental pillars of building trust is leading by example. As a leader, it is essential to demonstrate integrity and consistently adhere to your values and principles. By aligning your actions with your words, you create a sense of authenticity that resonates with others, garnering their trust and confidence in your leadership abilities. Remember, people are more likely to follow those they perceive as genuine and reliable.

Communication is another vital aspect of building trust. Effective leaders are excellent communicators who actively listen to their followers and respond with empathy and understanding. By fostering open lines of communication, you create an environment that encourages collaboration and transparency, further bolstering trust. Regularly providing updates, soliciting feedback, and addressing concerns will demonstrate your commitment to fostering a culture of trust and confidence.

Responsible Choices, Resilient Leaders: Navigating Campus Life with Integrity

In addition to leading by example and effective communication, establishing clear expectations is crucial. Clearly articulating your vision, goals, and values allows your followers to understand your leadership approach and what is expected of them. When everyone is on the same page, it becomes easier to build trust and confidence in your leadership, as they will know what to expect and how to contribute to the collective success.

Furthermore, cultivating healthy and positive relationships is essential to building trust. Treat everyone with respect, regardless of their position or background. Be approachable, empathetic, and supportive, creating a safe space for others to express their thoughts and concerns. Encouraging teamwork and collaboration will also foster a sense of trust and confidence in your leadership, as individuals feel valued and included.

Lastly, remember the importance of self-reflection and personal growth. Continuously evaluate your leadership style and seek feedback from others to identify areas for improvement. By demonstrating a commitment to personal development, you inspire confidence in your ability to lead effectively and adapt to the ever-changing needs of your followers.

In conclusion, building trust and confidence in your leadership is a continuous journey that requires self-awareness, authenticity, effective communication, clear expectations, positive relationships, and personal growth. By embodying these principles and strategies, you will be well on your way to becoming a resilient leader who not only achieves success but also inspires others to do the same. Remember, trust is the currency of leadership, and with it, you can navigate campus life with integrity and make responsible choices that positively impact your community while maintaining a strong relationship with God.

Conflict Resolution and Decision-Making

Responsible Choices, Resilient Leaders: Navigating Campus Life with Integrity

In the journey of becoming an aspiring leader on campus, it is crucial to develop effective conflict resolution and decision-making skills. As leaders, we are often faced with challenging situations that require us to navigate through conflicts and make tough choices. By mastering these skills, we can not only achieve success but also foster healthy relationships, maintain integrity, and make responsible choices that align with our values and beliefs.

Conflict resolution is an essential skill that allows us to address and resolve disagreements in a constructive manner. Conflict is inevitable, but how we handle it determines the outcome. As aspiring leaders, it is important to approach conflicts with an open mind and a willingness to listen to different perspectives. By actively seeking to understand others' viewpoints, we can find common ground and work towards a mutually beneficial resolution. Effective communication, empathy, and compromise are the pillars of conflict resolution, helping us build bridges and strengthen relationships rather than burn bridges and create animosity.

Decision-making, on the other hand, is a skill that requires thoughtful consideration and clarity of purpose. As leaders, we are faced with countless choices that impact not only ourselves but also those around us. To make responsible choices, we must assess the situation, gather information, and weigh the potential consequences. Having a strong moral compass is crucial in decision-making, as it helps us align our choices with our values and principles.

To enhance our decision-making abilities, it is essential to cultivate effective study habits and time management skills. By prioritizing and organizing our tasks, we can make informed decisions that maximize our productivity and minimize stress. Additionally, maintaining sobriety and healthy relationships contributes to our overall well-being and clarity of mind, enabling us to make sound choices.

(c) 2024: Responsible Choices, Resilient Leaders: Navigating Campus Life with Integrity

A serious relationship with God can provide guidance and strength as we navigate through conflicts and make decisions. Seeking spiritual wisdom and guidance can help us find inner peace and clarity in the face of challenges. By aligning our choices with our faith and values, we can lead with integrity and inspire others to do the same.

In conclusion, becoming an effective leader on campus requires honing conflict resolution and decision-making skills. By approaching conflicts with openness and empathy, and making thoughtful choices that align with our values and beliefs, we can create a positive impact, foster healthy relationships, and achieve success. Cultivating effective study habits, time management, sobriety, healthy relationships, responsible choices, and a serious relationship with God can further enhance our leadership journey. Remember, as aspiring leaders, our decisions and actions shape not only our own lives but also the lives of those around us.

Empowering and Supporting Others

Aspiring leaders, one of the most important aspects of leadership is the ability to empower and support others. In order to achieve success in your role on campus, it is crucial to understand the significance of building strong relationships, fostering a sense of belonging, and creating an environment that allows individuals to thrive. This subchapter delves into the importance of empowering and supporting others, providing you with strategies and insights to become a resilient leader.

When it comes to empowering others, it is essential to recognize the unique strengths and talents that each individual brings to the table. By acknowledging and appreciating these qualities, you can create an inclusive and collaborative environment where everyone feels valued and motivated to contribute their best. Encouraging open communication, active listening, and promoting teamwork are powerful ways to empower those around you.

Responsible Choices, Resilient Leaders: Navigating Campus Life with Integrity

Supporting others is equally important in leadership. By offering guidance, mentorship, and resources, you can help individuals overcome challenges and reach their full potential. Being a supportive leader means being approachable, understanding, and willing to lend a helping hand. This includes providing constructive feedback, offering advice, and being a source of encouragement during difficult times.

Furthermore, fostering a culture of empowerment and support goes hand in hand with promoting healthy relationships. By fostering positive connections among your peers, you can create a network of individuals who uplift and inspire one another. This not only enhances personal growth but also creates a supportive community that is essential for a successful college experience.

In addition, as a leader, it is crucial to lead by example and demonstrate integrity in all your actions. Upholding moral values, making responsible choices, and maintaining a serious relationship with God are key elements in building trust and respect among your peers. Your authenticity and commitment to living a virtuous life will inspire others to do the same.

Remember, true leadership is not about exerting power or authority over others, but rather about empowering and supporting them to become the best versions of themselves. By embracing these principles, you will not only achieve personal success but also create a positive impact on your campus community.

(c) 2024: Responsible Choices, Resilient Leaders: Navigating Campus Life with Integrity

In conclusion, empowering and supporting others is a fundamental aspect of effective leadership. By recognizing the unique strengths of individuals, fostering a sense of belonging, and creating a supportive environment, aspiring leaders can cultivate a culture of empowerment and growth on campus. Through this, you will not only achieve personal success but also inspire and uplift those around you, leaving a lasting impact on your campus community.

Chapter 5: Sobriety: Making Healthy Choices in a Campus Environment

Understanding the Risks and Consequences of Substance Abuse

As aspiring leaders, it is crucial to have a comprehensive understanding of the risks and consequences associated with substance abuse. Substance abuse refers to the harmful or excessive use of drugs or alcohol, which can have devastating effects on individuals, communities, and society as a whole. In this subchapter, we will delve into the various aspects of substance abuse, highlighting why it is essential for leaders to be well-informed about this issue.

First and foremost, substance abuse poses significant health risks. Regular and excessive consumption of drugs or alcohol can lead to physical and mental health problems, including liver damage, heart disease, addiction, depression, and anxiety. Such health issues can hamper one's ability to perform at their best, hindering their potential as leaders and affecting their overall well-being.

Responsible Choices, Resilient Leaders: Navigating Campus Life with Integrity

Furthermore, substance abuse can have severe consequences on academic and professional success. Engaging in substance abuse can lead to poor academic performance, missed deadlines, and lack of focus, ultimately jeopardizing one's academic and career goals. Aspiring leaders must realize that success is built on discipline, perseverance, and a sound mind, all of which can be compromised when substance abuse becomes a part of one's life.

Additionally, substance abuse can negatively impact relationships. Maintaining healthy relationships is crucial for leaders, as they often rely on the support and collaboration of others to accomplish their goals. Substance abuse can strain relationships with friends, family members, and colleagues, eroding trust and creating distance. It can also lead to isolation and a sense of alienation, making it difficult for aspiring leaders to build strong networks and inspire those around them.

Lastly, substance abuse carries legal and societal consequences. Engaging in illegal drug use or underage drinking can result in criminal charges, leading to legal troubles that can severely impede one's personal and professional growth. Moreover, substance abuse contributes to the larger societal issue of addiction and its associated problems, such as crime, poverty, and broken families. As leaders, it is our responsibility to contribute positively to society and advocate for healthier communities.

In conclusion, understanding the risks and consequences of substance abuse is vital for aspiring leaders. By being well-informed about this issue, leaders can make responsible choices, maintain their physical and mental well-being, achieve academic and professional success, foster healthy relationships, and contribute positively to society. As we navigate campus life with integrity, let us remember that sobriety, morality, healthy relationships, responsible choices, and a serious relationship with God are the pillars upon which our leadership journey should be built.

(c) 2024: Responsible Choices, Resilient Leaders: Navigating Campus Life with Integrity

Responsible Choices, Resilient Leaders: Navigating Campus Life with Integrity

Developing Personal Strategies for Sobriety

In the journey towards becoming a resilient leader on campus, one crucial aspect that aspiring leaders should pay attention to is their personal sobriety. Sobriety not only refers to abstaining from alcohol or drugs but also encompasses maintaining a clear and focused mindset in all areas of life. By developing personal strategies for sobriety, aspiring leaders can enhance their ability to make responsible choices, foster healthy relationships, and achieve success through effective study habits and time management.

1. Define your personal values: Begin by understanding what sobriety means to you and how it aligns with your personal values. Reflect on the reasons why sobriety is important to you and how it contributes to your overall well-being and success. This self-reflection will provide a solid foundation for developing strategies to maintain sobriety.

2. Surround yourself with supportive individuals: Seek out like-minded individuals who share your commitment to sobriety and personal growth. Surrounding yourself with a supportive network of friends, mentors, or campus organizations can provide encouragement and accountability as you navigate the challenges of college life.

3. Establish and maintain healthy routines: Create a daily routine that prioritizes activities that contribute to your sobriety and overall well-being. This may include allocating time for exercise, practicing mindfulness or meditation, engaging in hobbies or interests, and setting aside dedicated study time. By incorporating these activities into your routine, you can cultivate a balanced and fulfilling lifestyle that supports your sobriety goals.

4. Develop effective stress-management techniques: College life can be demanding, and stress is often a trigger for unhealthy coping mechanisms. Explore various stress-management techniques such as deep breathing exercises, journaling, or seeking professional counseling. By identifying and implementing healthy ways to manage stress, you can reduce the likelihood of turning to substances as a means of escape.

5. Seek out resources and support systems: Familiarize yourself with the resources available on campus that promote sobriety and mental health. Many universities offer counseling services, support groups, or workshops focused on substance abuse prevention. Taking advantage of these resources can provide valuable tools and guidance as you navigate the challenges of maintaining sobriety.

Remember, developing personal strategies for sobriety is an ongoing process. It requires commitment, self-reflection, and a willingness to adapt as circumstances change. By prioritizing your sobriety and making responsible choices, you will not only enhance your leadership abilities but also inspire others to follow a similar path towards personal growth and success.

Navigating Peer Pressure and Social Situations

As an aspiring leader on campus, it is important to understand how to navigate peer pressure and social situations while maintaining your integrity. College life often presents numerous opportunities to engage in activities that may not align with your personal values or goals. However, by developing effective strategies and a strong sense of self, you can successfully overcome these challenges and emerge as a resilient leader.

Responsible Choices, Resilient Leaders: Navigating Campus Life with Integrity

One of the key aspects of navigating peer pressure is developing a strong sense of self-awareness. It is essential to understand your values, beliefs, and goals before entering any social situation. By doing so, you can make informed decisions that align with your principles and avoid succumbing to peer pressure. Remember that being a leader does not mean sacrificing your values; it means standing up for what you believe in, even in the face of adversity.

Effective communication skills are also crucial when dealing with peer pressure and social situations. Learn to express your thoughts and opinions confidently and respectfully. This will not only help you assert your boundaries, but also allow you to engage in meaningful discussions and challenge societal norms when necessary. Surround yourself with like-minded individuals who support your goals and aspirations, as they will provide a strong foundation of support.

Time management is another vital skill for aspiring leaders. Balancing academic responsibilities, extracurricular activities, and social engagements can be challenging, but it is crucial for success. Set realistic goals, prioritize tasks, and develop a schedule that allows for productive studying, self-care, and socializing. By managing your time effectively, you can avoid succumbing to peer pressure due to time constraints or feeling overwhelmed.

Furthermore, maintaining sobriety and making responsible choices is essential for aspiring leaders. Engaging in risky behaviors such as excessive drinking or drug use can negatively impact academic performance, relationships, and personal well-being. Instead, focus on healthy habits, such as exercise, mindfulness, and seeking support from friends and mentors. By making responsible choices, you demonstrate your commitment to personal growth and become a role model for others.

Finally, nurturing a serious relationship with God can provide a strong foundation for your leadership journey. Develop spiritual practices that align with your beliefs and engage in regular reflection and self-examination. This connection will not only provide guidance and strength during challenging times but also help you develop empathy, compassion, and a sense of purpose.

In conclusion, navigating peer pressure and social situations is an essential skill for aspiring leaders. By developing self-awareness, effective communication skills, time management abilities, and making responsible choices, you can maintain your integrity while achieving success on campus. Additionally, nurturing a serious relationship with God will provide a solid foundation for your leadership journey. Remember, being a leader means staying true to your values and making responsible choices that positively impact your personal growth and the community around you.

Finding Support and Resources for Recovery

In the journey of life, we all encounter challenges and obstacles that test our resilience and character. As aspiring leaders, it is crucial to recognize the importance of finding support and resources for recovery. Whether we are facing personal struggles, addiction, or mental health issues, seeking assistance is a sign of strength, not weakness. In this subchapter, we will explore the various avenues available to us to navigate the path to recovery and achieve success in our roles as leaders on campus.

First and foremost, it is essential to acknowledge that we do not have to face our challenges alone. There are numerous support systems and resources available within our campus community. Counseling services, support groups, and peer mentorship programs can provide invaluable guidance, understanding, and encouragement. These resources can help us develop effective coping strategies, enhance our self-awareness, and foster personal growth.

Additionally, reaching out to trusted faculty members, advisors, or campus chaplains can offer a compassionate ear and guidance in times of need. These individuals can provide mentorship, wisdom, and spiritual support, helping us navigate the intricate web of responsibilities and choices that come with leadership positions.

While seeking support from others is crucial, it is equally important to cultivate self-care practices. Building a routine that includes healthy habits, such as regular exercise, proper nutrition, and sufficient sleep, can significantly contribute to our overall well-being and resilience. Taking time for ourselves, engaging in hobbies, and practicing mindfulness can also help us manage stress and maintain a healthy work-life balance.

Furthermore, as aspiring leaders, we must recognize that recovery is an ongoing process. It requires commitment, perseverance, and a serious relationship with ourselves and a higher power. Cultivating a spiritual practice, whether it be through prayer, meditation, or engaging in religious activities, can provide a sense of purpose, guidance, and strength.

In conclusion, finding support and resources for recovery is an essential aspect of our journey as aspiring leaders. By actively seeking assistance, we demonstrate our commitment to personal growth, integrity, and responsible choices. Through counseling services, support groups, mentorship, self-care practices, and a serious relationship with ourselves and a higher power, we can navigate the challenges of campus life, achieve success, and become resilient leaders with integrity. Remember, a strong leader is not one who never falls but one who rises after every fall.

Promoting a Culture of Responsibility and Sobriety on Campus

Responsible Choices, Resilient Leaders: Navigating Campus Life with Integrity

As aspiring leaders, it is crucial to recognize the importance of promoting a culture of responsibility and sobriety on campus. In the pursuit of success, effective study habits, time management, leadership, sobriety, morality, healthy relationships, responsible choices, and a serious relationship with God are all integral aspects of a well-rounded student experience.

One of the key elements of promoting responsibility and sobriety is fostering a supportive environment that encourages healthy choices. This begins with cultivating a strong sense of personal responsibility among students. By emphasizing the importance of making responsible choices, students can develop the necessary skills and awareness to navigate the challenges of campus life. This includes encouraging students to prioritize their academic responsibilities, manage their time effectively, and maintain a healthy work-life balance.

Moreover, it is essential to address the issue of substance abuse on campus. Encouraging sobriety not only promotes a safer environment but also allows students to fully engage in their academic and personal growth. By raising awareness about the risks and consequences associated with substance abuse, aspiring leaders can help students make informed decisions regarding their health and well-being.

Morality and ethical behavior are also integral to fostering a culture of responsibility. As leaders, it is important to exemplify and promote honesty, integrity, and respect for others. By encouraging students to embrace these values, aspiring leaders can create a positive and inclusive atmosphere on campus, where individuals feel valued and respected.

(c) 2024: Responsible Choices, Resilient Leaders: Navigating Campus Life with Integrity

Healthy relationships play a vital role in a student's overall well-being. By promoting healthy relationship dynamics and providing resources for conflict resolution and communication skills, aspiring leaders can help students cultivate meaningful connections. These relationships contribute to a supportive community that encourages responsible decision-making and personal growth.

Lastly, a serious relationship with God can provide a solid foundation for responsible choices and personal development. By encouraging students to explore and strengthen their faith, aspiring leaders can help them find solace, guidance, and purpose in their journey.

In conclusion, promoting a culture of responsibility and sobriety on campus is essential for aspiring leaders. By emphasizing effective study habits, time management, leadership, sobriety, morality, healthy relationships, responsible choices, and a serious relationship with God, students can develop into resilient leaders who excel academically and personally. Through their commitment to these principles, aspiring leaders can create a campus environment that fosters growth, integrity, and a strong sense of community.

Chapter 6: Morality and Ethics: Making Ethical Decisions in Campus Life

Understanding Personal Values and Beliefs

In order to become effective leaders on campus and achieve success in all areas of life, aspiring leaders must first understand and define their personal values and beliefs. Our personal values and beliefs shape our character, guide our decisions, and determine our actions. They are the foundation upon which we build our lives and the compass that directs us towards our goals.

Responsible Choices, Resilient Leaders: Navigating Campus Life with Integrity

Personal values are the principles and standards by which we live our lives. They reflect what we consider to be important and determine our priorities. Our values may include integrity, honesty, compassion, respect, responsibility, and many others. These values serve as the moral compass that guides our actions and behaviors, both in our personal and professional lives. Understanding our personal values helps us make responsible choices and act with integrity, even in challenging situations.

Beliefs, on the other hand, are our deeply held convictions about the world, ourselves, and others. They shape our perceptions, attitudes, and behaviors. Our beliefs can be influenced by our upbringing, cultural background, education, and personal experiences. They play a crucial role in how we interpret and respond to events and situations. By understanding and analyzing our beliefs, we can identify any biases or limitations that may hinder our growth as leaders.

To develop a clear understanding of our personal values and beliefs, it is vital to take the time for self-reflection and introspection. This involves asking ourselves thought-provoking questions such as: What principles do I hold dear? What do I stand for? What kind of person do I aspire to be? What are my core beliefs about leadership, success, and relationships? By delving deep into these questions, we can gain clarity about our values and beliefs, enabling us to align our actions with our principles.

Additionally, cultivating a serious relationship with God can provide a solid foundation for our personal values and beliefs. Seeking guidance from a higher power and living according to spiritual principles can strengthen our moral compass and provide us with the strength and resilience to overcome challenges. It also allows us to connect with others who share similar values and beliefs, fostering healthy relationships and a sense of community.

(c) 2024: Responsible Choices, Resilient Leaders: Navigating Campus Life with Integrity

Responsible Choices, Resilient Leaders: Navigating Campus Life with Integrity

Understanding personal values and beliefs is essential for aspiring leaders who aim to make responsible choices and navigate campus life with integrity. By identifying and aligning our actions with our values and beliefs, we can cultivate success not only in our academic pursuits but also in our relationships, leadership roles, and personal growth journeys.

Ethical Dilemmas on Campus and How to Navigate Them

In the fast-paced and diverse environment of campus life, aspiring leaders often find themselves facing various ethical dilemmas. These situations can arise in academic settings, social interactions, and personal choices. Navigating these ethical challenges with integrity is crucial for developing leadership skills and becoming a resilient leader. In this subchapter, we will explore some common ethical dilemmas on campus and provide guidance on how to approach them.

One prevalent ethical dilemma on campus is academic integrity. As aspiring leaders, it is essential to uphold honest and responsible behavior in all academic pursuits. This means avoiding plagiarism, cheating, or any form of dishonesty. Instead, focus on effective study habits and time management to achieve success in your academic endeavors. Seek help from professors, tutors, or study groups when needed, and prioritize your assignments and responsibilities to avoid the temptation of unethical behavior.

Another ethical dilemma that frequently arises on campus is the pressure to engage in unhealthy or immoral activities. As a leader, it is crucial to make responsible choices that align with your values and contribute positively to your personal growth. Avoid succumbing to the pressure of substance abuse, excessive partying, or engaging in activities that compromise your well-being. Sobriety and healthy relationships should be prioritized, as they contribute to your overall success and leadership development.

Navigating ethical dilemmas also requires a serious commitment to a personal relationship with God. Faith can provide a strong moral compass and guide your decision-making process. Cultivate a deep connection with your beliefs and values, allowing them to shape your choices and actions on campus. Seek support from campus religious organizations or spiritual mentors who can help you strengthen your relationship with God.

Ultimately, ethical dilemmas on campus can be challenging, but by embracing responsible choices and maintaining integrity, aspiring leaders can navigate these situations successfully. Remember, leadership is not only about achieving personal success but also about positively influencing those around you. By making ethical decisions, aspiring leaders can inspire others to do the same and foster a culture of integrity on campus.

In conclusion, this subchapter highlights the importance of addressing ethical dilemmas on campus and provides valuable insights on how to navigate them. As aspiring leaders, it is essential to cultivate effective study habits, practice time management, prioritize moral values, maintain healthy relationships, and make responsible choices. By incorporating these principles into your daily life and developing a strong relationship with God, you can become a resilient leader who upholds integrity and positively impacts your campus community.

Developing a Moral Compass for Decision-Making

In today's complex and fast-paced world, the ability to make responsible choices is a crucial skill for aspiring leaders. As you navigate campus life and strive for success, it is essential to develop a moral compass that guides your decision-making. In this subchapter, we will explore the importance of morality and how it can shape your leadership journey.

Responsible Choices, Resilient Leaders: Navigating Campus Life with Integrity

Morality is the foundation upon which integrity is built. It is the inner compass that directs us towards making choices that align with our values and principles. As a leader, your actions and decisions have a ripple effect on those around you, and having a strong moral compass will enable you to make ethically sound choices that inspire and motivate others.

To develop a moral compass, start by reflecting on your core values. What principles do you hold dear? What kind of person do you aspire to be? By understanding your values, you can establish a framework for decision-making that is rooted in integrity.

Once you have identified your values, it is crucial to consistently practice them in your daily life. This requires self-awareness and a commitment to align your actions with your beliefs. Engage in regular self-reflection to assess whether your decisions are in line with your moral compass. Seek feedback from trusted mentors or friends who can provide honest insights into your behavior.

Another crucial aspect of developing a moral compass is empathy. Understanding the perspectives and feelings of others allows you to make decisions that consider the well-being of everyone involved. Cultivate your ability to listen and understand different viewpoints, even if they differ from your own. This will help you make inclusive and fair choices that promote a healthy and supportive campus community.

Lastly, fostering a relationship with a higher power can provide a solid foundation for your moral compass. Whether it is through prayer, meditation, or connecting with a spiritual community, nurturing your faith can provide guidance and strength in times of moral dilemmas.

(c) 2024: Responsible Choices, Resilient Leaders: Navigating Campus Life with Integrity

In conclusion, developing a moral compass is essential for aspiring leaders who seek to make responsible choices and achieve success. By understanding your core values, practicing them consistently, cultivating empathy, and nurturing your spiritual connection, you can navigate campus life with integrity. As you make choices aligned with your moral compass, you inspire others to do the same, creating a campus culture that fosters healthy relationships, responsible choices, and resilient leadership.

Promoting Integrity and Honesty in Campus Interactions

In today's fast-paced and highly competitive world, aspiring leaders must possess not only the necessary skills and knowledge but also a strong foundation of integrity and honesty. The ability to navigate campus life with integrity is crucial for achieving success and making responsible choices. In this subchapter, we will explore the importance of promoting integrity and honesty in campus interactions, and how it contributes to becoming a resilient leader.

Integrity is the quality of being honest and having strong moral principles. It means consistently acting in accordance with one's values, regardless of the circumstances. As aspiring leaders, it is essential to cultivate integrity in all aspects of our lives, including our campus interactions. Honesty, on the other hand, involves being truthful, transparent, and accountable for our actions. Together, integrity and honesty lay the foundation for building trust and credibility with our peers, professors, and the entire campus community.

One of the key ways to promote integrity and honesty in campus interactions is by leading by example. As aspiring leaders, we must demonstrate these qualities in our daily lives, both in and out of the classroom. This means being punctual, meeting deadlines, and fulfilling commitments. It also involves avoiding academic dishonesty, such as plagiarism or cheating, and encouraging others to do the same.

Another important aspect of promoting integrity and honesty is fostering a culture of open communication and mutual respect. Creating an environment where individuals feel comfortable expressing their thoughts and concerns without fear of judgment or reprisal is crucial. As leaders, we should actively listen, provide constructive feedback, and promote inclusivity, ensuring that all voices are heard and respected.

Furthermore, promoting integrity and honesty involves embracing diversity and cultivating healthy relationships. Respecting and valuing the differences among individuals fosters an atmosphere of trust and understanding. By promoting inclusivity and appreciating different perspectives, we create an environment that encourages honesty and integrity in all campus interactions.

Lastly, cultivating a serious relationship with God can serve as a guiding force in promoting integrity and honesty. Faith provides a moral compass and helps us make responsible choices that align with our values. By seeking guidance from our faith, we can navigate the challenges of campus life with integrity and remain steadfast in our commitment to honesty.

In conclusion, promoting integrity and honesty in campus interactions is crucial for aspiring leaders. By leading by example, fostering open communication, embracing diversity, and cultivating a serious relationship with God, we can create a campus environment where integrity and honesty are valued and practiced. Navigating campus life with integrity not only helps us achieve success through effective study habits and time management but also strengthens our moral character, making us resilient leaders prepared to make responsible choices in all aspects of life.

Fostering a Culture of Ethical Behavior and Accountability

Responsible Choices, Resilient Leaders: Navigating Campus Life with Integrity

Aspiring leaders play a critical role in shaping the culture of their campus community. By setting an example of ethical behavior and promoting accountability, they can create an environment that fosters success, personal growth, and a sense of responsibility. In this subchapter, we will explore the importance of cultivating a culture of ethical behavior and accountability, and how it aligns with the values of effective study habits, time management, leadership, sobriety, morality, healthy relationships, responsible choices, and a serious relationship with God.

Ethical behavior forms the foundation of any thriving community. It is about conducting oneself with integrity, honesty, and respect for others. As leaders, it is crucial to demonstrate these qualities in our actions and decisions. By consistently upholding ethical standards, we inspire others to follow suit and create a positive ripple effect on campus.

Accountability goes hand in hand with ethical behavior. It involves taking ownership of our actions, acknowledging our mistakes, and learning from them. As aspiring leaders, we must hold ourselves accountable and encourage others to do the same. This means being responsible for our commitments, meeting deadlines, and fulfilling obligations. When we promote accountability, we create an environment where trust and reliability thrive, enhancing the overall campus experience.

To foster a culture of ethical behavior and accountability, it is essential to lead by example. By consistently demonstrating our commitment to these values, we inspire others to do the same. We can achieve this by practicing effective study habits, managing our time efficiently, and prioritizing our responsibilities. When we show dedication and discipline in our academic pursuits, we encourage our peers to do the same, creating a culture that values education and personal growth.

A focus on sobriety, morality, and healthy relationships is also crucial to fostering ethical behavior and accountability. By making responsible choices regarding substance use, treating others with kindness and respect, and maintaining healthy boundaries within our relationships, we create an environment that promotes personal well-being and encourages others to do the same.

Finally, our journey towards fostering a culture of ethical behavior and accountability is deeply intertwined with our relationship with God. By cultivating a serious and genuine connection with our faith, we gain the strength, wisdom, and guidance to navigate the complexities of leadership with integrity. Our faith serves as a compass, guiding us to make responsible choices and upholding ethical standards in all aspects of our lives.

In conclusion, aspiring leaders have the power to create a culture of ethical behavior and accountability on campus. By leading by example, promoting responsibility and integrity, and nurturing our relationship with God, we can inspire others to embrace these values. In doing so, we contribute to a campus environment that values personal growth, success, and the well-being of all its members.

Chapter 7: Building Healthy Relationships: Nurturing Connections on Campus

Understanding the Importance of Healthy Relationships

In the journey of becoming a resilient leader on campus, one cannot underestimate the significance of cultivating healthy relationships. Aspiring leaders must recognize that their success is not solely dependent on their individual achievements, but also on the support and collaboration they receive from those around them. Therefore, understanding the importance of healthy relationships is paramount.

Responsible Choices, Resilient Leaders: Navigating Campus Life with Integrity

Healthy relationships are built on trust, respect, and effective communication. These qualities are fundamental in fostering an environment where ideas can be freely shared, conflicts can be resolved amicably, and collaboration can thrive. As an aspiring leader, it is crucial to surround yourself with individuals who inspire and challenge you to grow, both personally and professionally.

When we engage in healthy relationships, we create a supportive network that can help us navigate the challenges of campus life. This network can be a source of emotional support during times of stress or uncertainty. By fostering positive connections, we can lean on each other for encouragement, guidance, and motivation.

Furthermore, healthy relationships contribute to personal development. Interacting with diverse individuals allows us to gain new perspectives, broaden our horizons, and develop empathy. These qualities are key to effective leadership, as they enable us to understand and connect with a variety of people, leading to more inclusive and equitable decision-making processes.

In addition to personal growth, healthy relationships also contribute to academic success. Surrounding yourself with like-minded individuals who prioritize effective study habits and time management can provide a supportive structure for achieving academic goals. These relationships can serve as accountability partners, encouraging each other to stay focused, motivated, and on track.

Lastly, aspiring leaders who prioritize healthy relationships are more likely to make responsible choices and maintain a balanced lifestyle. By surrounding ourselves with individuals who value sobriety, morality, and responsible choices, we are more likely to be influenced positively. These relationships can help us resist negative peer pressure, make informed decisions, and maintain a healthy work-life balance.

(c) 2024: Responsible Choices, Resilient Leaders: Navigating Campus Life with Integrity

Responsible Choices, Resilient Leaders: Navigating Campus Life with Integrity

In conclusion, aspiring leaders must recognize the profound impact that healthy relationships can have on their personal and professional growth. By cultivating relationships based on trust, respect, and effective communication, leaders create a supportive network that fosters emotional well-being, personal development, academic success, and responsible choices. As you embark on your journey towards leadership, prioritize healthy relationships and surround yourself with individuals who inspire and challenge you to become the best version of yourself.

Communication Skills for Building Strong Connections

In order to become an effective leader on campus and achieve success in all aspects of your life, it is crucial to develop strong communication skills. Building strong connections with others is essential for fostering healthy relationships, promoting teamwork, and creating a positive impact on campus. This subchapter will provide you with valuable insights and strategies to enhance your communication skills and cultivate meaningful connections.

Effective communication is more than just conveying information; it involves active listening, empathy, and understanding. As an aspiring leader, you must learn to listen attentively to others, valuing their opinions and perspectives. By practicing active listening, you will encourage open dialogue, foster trust, and demonstrate respect for others' ideas.

Empathy is another vital aspect of communication skills. Putting yourself in someone else's shoes allows you to understand their emotions and experiences, leading to more meaningful connections. By showing empathy, you will create a supportive and inclusive environment that encourages others to share their thoughts and concerns.

Responsible Choices, Resilient Leaders: Navigating Campus Life with Integrity

Furthermore, understanding non-verbal cues is essential for effective communication. Pay attention to body language, facial expressions, and tone of voice – they often convey more than words alone. Being aware of these cues will help you respond appropriately and build stronger connections.

Additionally, it is crucial to communicate assertively and respectfully. Expressing your thoughts and ideas clearly and confidently, while still considering others' viewpoints, empowers you as a leader. By practicing assertive communication, you will inspire others to do the same, creating an environment of mutual respect and collaboration.

Technology plays a significant role in communication today, but it is important not to neglect face-to-face interactions. Engaging in meaningful conversations, whether through group discussions, one-on-one meetings, or campus events, allows you to build genuine connections with your peers and mentors. Remember, effective communication is a two-way street – it involves both speaking and listening.

Lastly, building strong connections also requires being authentic and genuine. Showcasing your true self, expressing your values, and being reliable will attract like-minded individuals and foster deeper connections based on trust and shared aspirations.

In conclusion, mastering communication skills is crucial for aspiring leaders. By actively listening, practicing empathy, understanding non-verbal cues, communicating assertively, engaging in face-to-face interactions, and being authentic, you will be well-equipped to build strong connections on campus. These skills will not only enhance your ability to lead effectively but also contribute to your personal growth and success in all areas of life. Remember, communication is the foundation for meaningful relationships and a key element in navigating campus life with integrity.

Developing Empathy and Emotional Intelligence

Responsible Choices, Resilient Leaders: Navigating Campus Life with Integrity

In the journey towards becoming a successful leader on campus, it is crucial to recognize the significance of developing empathy and emotional intelligence. These two qualities go hand in hand and serve as essential tools for navigating campus life with integrity. As aspiring leaders, it is our responsibility to cultivate these traits to not only succeed academically but also to foster healthy relationships, make responsible choices, and lead a purposeful life.

Emotional intelligence encompasses the ability to identify, understand, and manage one's emotions, as well as being attuned to the emotions of others. It involves being self-aware, having self-regulation, showing empathy, and possessing good social skills. By honing these skills, we can better navigate the challenges of campus life and build stronger connections with our peers.

Empathy, on the other hand, is the ability to put ourselves in someone else's shoes and understand their feelings and perspectives. It allows us to connect with others on a deeper level, fostering trust and compassion. As aspiring leaders, empathy is crucial in building meaningful relationships, resolving conflicts, and creating a supportive environment for those around us.

Developing empathy and emotional intelligence starts with self-reflection. Take the time to understand your own emotions, triggers, and strengths. This awareness will enable you to regulate your emotions effectively and respond to situations in a more thoughtful and measured way. By becoming more attuned to your emotions, you can also better understand the emotions of others, allowing you to respond with empathy and kindness.

(c) 2024: Responsible Choices, Resilient Leaders: Navigating Campus Life with Integrity

Active listening is another key aspect of developing empathy. Truly listen to others without judgment or interruption. Try to understand their perspective, validate their feelings, and provide support when needed. This will not only strengthen your relationships but also create an environment of trust and openness.

Additionally, cultivating empathy and emotional intelligence requires practicing selflessness. Look beyond your own needs and desires and consider the well-being of others. Offer your support, lend a helping hand, and show genuine care for those around you. By doing so, you will foster a sense of community and inspire others to do the same.

In conclusion, developing empathy and emotional intelligence is instrumental in becoming a resilient leader on campus. It allows us to forge meaningful connections, make responsible choices, and create a positive impact within our communities. By cultivating these qualities, we not only enhance our personal growth but also contribute to the betterment of our campus environment. As aspiring leaders, let us strive to develop empathy and emotional intelligence, as these traits will guide us towards a successful and fulfilling journey through campus life.

Resolving Conflict and Building Trust

In the pursuit of becoming effective leaders on campus, one crucial skill that aspiring leaders must develop is the ability to resolve conflicts and build trust. Conflict is inevitable, and as leaders, it is our responsibility to address and resolve it in a manner that strengthens relationships and fosters a positive environment. Moreover, trust is the foundation of any successful team or organization, and without it, leadership becomes a mere title without influence.

Responsible Choices, Resilient Leaders: Navigating Campus Life with Integrity

To effectively resolve conflicts, aspiring leaders must first understand the root causes of the disagreement. Often, conflicts arise from misunderstandings, differing perspectives, or unmet expectations. By actively listening and seeking to understand the underlying issues, leaders can begin to find common ground and work towards a resolution. It is essential to approach conflicts with an open mind, empathy, and a willingness to compromise when necessary. By doing so, leaders can create an atmosphere of collaboration and cooperation, rather than one of division.

Building trust is a continuous process that requires consistency, honesty, and integrity. Aspiring leaders must lead by example and demonstrate their commitment to their values and principles. By acting in a manner that aligns with their words, leaders earn the trust and respect of their peers and followers. Additionally, leaders must be transparent in their decision-making process and communicate openly and honestly with others. Trust is built on a foundation of authenticity and reliability, and leaders must strive to be trustworthy in all their interactions.

In order to foster an environment of trust and conflict resolution, aspiring leaders must also prioritize healthy relationships. This includes developing strong communication skills, actively seeking feedback, and valuing the input of others. By creating an atmosphere where individuals feel heard and valued, leaders can encourage open dialogue and collaboration, leading to better problem-solving and decision-making.

Lastly, a serious relationship with God can greatly contribute to resolving conflicts and building trust. By seeking guidance from a higher power and relying on faith, leaders can approach conflicts with humility and forgiveness. Additionally, spiritual values can provide a moral compass, guiding leaders towards ethical and responsible choices.

(c) 2024: Responsible Choices, Resilient Leaders: Navigating Campus Life with Integrity

Responsible Choices, Resilient Leaders: Navigating Campus Life with Integrity

In conclusion, as aspiring leaders, it is imperative to develop the skills necessary to resolve conflicts and build trust. By actively seeking to understand conflicts, leading with integrity, fostering healthy relationships, and relying on a higher power, leaders can create an environment that encourages collaboration, trust, and growth. Embracing conflict resolution and trust-building strategies will not only contribute to personal success but also empower leaders to positively impact their campus and beyond.

Creating a Supportive and Inclusive Community

As an aspiring leader, one of the most important skills you can cultivate is the ability to create a supportive and inclusive community. In this subchapter, we will explore the vital role that a leader plays in fostering an environment that encourages success, promotes healthy relationships, and embraces diversity.

To begin, it is essential to recognize that a supportive and inclusive community is built on a foundation of respect and empathy. As a leader, it is your responsibility to lead by example and treat everyone with kindness and understanding. By embracing diversity and valuing different perspectives, you can create an environment where everyone feels valued and included.

Effective communication is also crucial in fostering a supportive community. Encourage open dialogue and active listening among your peers. By creating a safe space for individuals to express their thoughts and concerns, you can address issues and find solutions together. Remember, a supportive community is built on collaboration and understanding.

Furthermore, promoting healthy relationships is paramount to creating a supportive environment. Encourage your peers to build meaningful connections based on trust, respect, and shared values. By fostering a culture of inclusivity and belonging, you can help individuals develop a support system that will empower them to achieve their goals.

In addition to cultivating healthy relationships, it is important to encourage responsible choices and integrity within your community. As a leader, you have the opportunity to inspire others to make ethical decisions that align with their values. By setting a positive example and holding yourself accountable, you can inspire others to do the same.

Lastly, a serious relationship with God can provide a strong foundation for personal growth and leadership. Encourage your peers to explore their spirituality and seek guidance from their faith. By fostering a community that supports individual spiritual journeys, you can create a sense of purpose and fulfillment among your peers.

In conclusion, creating a supportive and inclusive community is a fundamental aspect of responsible leadership. By embodying respect, empathy, and integrity, you can foster an environment that promotes success, healthy relationships, and personal growth. Remember, as an aspiring leader, it is your duty to create a community where everyone feels valued, included, and empowered to make responsible choices.

Chapter 8: Responsible Choices: Making Sound Decisions in Campus Life

Assessing the Consequences of Choices and Actions

Responsible Choices, Resilient Leaders: Navigating Campus Life with Integrity

In the journey of becoming a leader on campus and achieving success, one must understand the significance of assessing the consequences of choices and actions. Every decision we make has an impact, not only on our own lives but also on the lives of those around us. It is crucial to recognize that responsible choices and actions can shape our future and determine the path we take in our personal and professional lives.

When we assess the consequences of our choices and actions, we gain a deeper understanding of the potential outcomes. This empowers us to make informed decisions, rather than acting impulsively or being swayed by external influences. By taking a moment to reflect on the potential impact of our choices, we can avoid making hasty decisions that may have detrimental effects on our goals, relationships, and overall well-being.

Effective study habits and time management play a vital role in assessing consequences. As aspiring leaders, it is essential to prioritize our academic commitments and allocate time wisely. By understanding the consequences of procrastination or poor study habits, we can avoid the stress and negative outcomes that result from lack of preparation. This not only enhances our academic performance but also allows us to develop essential skills such as discipline, focus, and perseverance.

Leadership, sobriety, morality, healthy relationships, and responsible choices are closely intertwined. Each decision we make in these areas has a ripple effect on our personal and professional lives. By assessing the potential consequences of our actions, we can make choices that align with our values and contribute to our overall growth and success as leaders. Whether it is choosing to lead by example, maintaining sobriety to stay focused and committed, or fostering healthy relationships built on trust and respect, our choices shape our character and influence those around us.

Lastly, a serious relationship with God can guide us in assessing the consequences of our choices and actions. By seeking wisdom and guidance from a higher power, we can make decisions that align with our moral compass and lead to positive outcomes. This spiritual connection can provide a sense of purpose, strength, and resilience as we navigate the challenges and opportunities of campus life.

In conclusion, assessing the consequences of choices and actions is a fundamental aspect of becoming a resilient leader. By understanding the potential outcomes of our decisions, we can make responsible choices that lead to success in academics, relationships, and personal growth. Through effective study habits, time management, leadership, sobriety, morality, healthy relationships, and a serious relationship with God, we can shape our future and positively impact the lives of those around us. Remember, the choices we make today determine the leaders we become tomorrow.

Recognizing Peer Influence and Making Independent Decisions

In the journey of becoming a resilient leader on campus, one of the most crucial skills to develop is the ability to recognize peer influence and make independent decisions. As aspiring leaders, we often find ourselves surrounded by a diverse group of individuals, each with their own set of values, beliefs, and habits. It is essential to navigate these influences wisely and stay true to our own principles in order to achieve success and make responsible choices.

Peer influence can be both positive and negative. On one hand, it can inspire us to strive for greatness, push our boundaries, and explore new perspectives. On the other hand, it can lead us astray from our goals, compromise our values, and hinder our personal growth. Recognizing these influences is the first step towards making independent decisions.

Responsible Choices, Resilient Leaders: Navigating Campus Life with Integrity

To navigate peer influence effectively, it is important to cultivate self-awareness. Take the time to reflect on your own values, goals, and aspirations. Understand what truly matters to you and what you want to achieve during your time on campus. This self-awareness will serve as a compass, guiding you towards making decisions that align with your personal vision and values.

Seek out like-minded individuals who share your values and goals. Surrounding yourself with positive influences will not only reinforce your own commitment but also provide a support system that encourages your growth as a leader. These individuals can serve as mentors, accountability partners, and sources of inspiration.

However, it is equally important to be open to diverse perspectives and experiences. Engage in meaningful conversations with peers who may hold different beliefs and opinions. This will broaden your understanding of the world, challenge your assumptions, and help you develop empathy and critical thinking skills. By actively listening and considering different perspectives, you can make informed decisions that are not solely influenced by the opinions of others.

Remember that being a resilient leader means being able to stand firm in your own convictions while respecting the choices of others. It is essential to strike a balance between asserting your own values and beliefs and fostering an inclusive and respectful environment. By doing so, you can create healthy relationships based on trust and mutual understanding.

(c) 2024: Responsible Choices, Resilient Leaders: Navigating Campus Life with Integrity

Responsible Choices, Resilient Leaders: Navigating Campus Life with Integrity

Ultimately, recognizing peer influence and making independent decisions is a lifelong skill that goes beyond campus life. It is a key characteristic of a resilient leader who is able to navigate various challenges and make responsible choices in all aspects of life. So, embrace the power of influence, but always remember to stay true to yourself and forge your own path towards success, integrity, and a meaningful relationship with God.

Seeking Guidance and Mentorship for Decision-Making

In the journey of becoming a leader on campus and achieving success in all areas of your life, there is no denying the importance of seeking guidance and mentorship for decision-making. As aspiring leaders, we often find ourselves faced with difficult choices that can impact not only our personal lives but also the lives of those around us. It is during these times that guidance and mentorship become invaluable tools to help us navigate the complexities of decision-making with integrity.

One of the most effective ways to seek guidance is by finding a mentor who embodies the qualities and values you aspire to possess. A mentor is someone who has walked the path you wish to follow and can provide invaluable insights and wisdom gained from their own experiences. Look for individuals who have excelled in areas such as effective study habits, time management, leadership, sobriety, morality, healthy relationships, responsible choices, and a serious relationship with God. Seek out their guidance and learn from their successes and failures, allowing their wisdom to shape your own decision-making process.

In addition to finding a mentor, it is crucial to develop a habit of seeking guidance from God. Cultivating a serious relationship with God not only provides a moral compass but also opens doors to divine guidance and wisdom. Through prayer and reflection, you can find solace in seeking God's will and allowing His guidance to influence your decision-making.

It is important to remember that seeking guidance does not mean relinquishing your autonomy or decision-making abilities. Instead, it is a recognition of the power of wisdom and the value of learning from those who have gone before us. It is about leveraging the collective experiences of others to make informed, responsible choices that align with your own values and goals.

While seeking guidance and mentorship is essential, it is equally important to approach these relationships with humility, gratitude, and a willingness to learn. Be open to constructive criticism and feedback, for it is through these interactions that personal growth occurs. Embrace the opportunity to expand your perspective and consider alternative viewpoints, as this will ultimately strengthen your decision-making abilities.

In conclusion, seeking guidance and mentorship for decision-making is a crucial aspect of becoming a responsible and resilient leader. Through the guidance of mentors and a serious relationship with God, you can navigate the complexities of decision-making with integrity and make responsible choices that align with your values and goals. Embrace the wisdom of others, remain humble, and approach these relationships with gratitude, for they will play a significant role in shaping the leader you aspire to be. Remember, the journey towards success is not meant to be taken alone, and seeking guidance is a powerful tool that will propel you towards achieving your aspirations.

Resisting Negative Influences and Temptations

As aspiring leaders on campus, it is crucial to develop the strength and resilience to resist negative influences and temptations that may hinder your personal growth and success. In a world filled with distractions and vices, it is essential to stay focused on your goals and maintain your integrity. This subchapter will provide you with valuable insights and practical strategies to navigate these challenges and make responsible choices that align with your values and aspirations.

Responsible Choices, Resilient Leaders: Navigating Campus Life with Integrity

One of the first steps in resisting negative influences is to understand your own values and beliefs. Take the time to reflect on what is truly important to you and what you stand for as a leader. By having a clear vision of your principles, you will be better equipped to make decisions that are in line with your personal and professional goals.

Additionally, it is essential to surround yourself with positive and like-minded individuals who share your values. Seek out mentors and friends who inspire you to be the best version of yourself and who will support you in your quest for success. Building healthy relationships based on mutual respect, trust, and accountability will not only provide you with a support system but also help you resist negative influences.

Furthermore, effective time management and study habits are key to staying focused and achieving academic success. Prioritize your commitments and create a schedule that allows for dedicated study time. By staying organized and disciplined, you can minimize the likelihood of succumbing to distractions and temptations.

As you strive to resist negative influences, sobriety plays a significant role. Understand the potential consequences of substance abuse and the impact it can have on your personal and academic life. Embrace a healthy lifestyle that includes regular exercise, proper nutrition, and adequate sleep. By taking care of your physical and mental well-being, you will be better equipped to make responsible choices and resist temptations.

Lastly, cultivating a serious relationship with God can provide you with guidance and strength in your journey as a leader. Find time for prayer, meditation, and reflection to nourish your spiritual growth. This connection with a higher power can serve as a source of inspiration and resilience during challenging times.

(c) 2024: Responsible Choices, Resilient Leaders: Navigating Campus Life with Integrity

In conclusion, resisting negative influences and temptations is a crucial aspect of becoming a responsible and resilient leader. By understanding your values, surrounding yourself with positive influences, managing your time effectively, maintaining sobriety, and nurturing a relationship with God, you will be better equipped to make responsible choices and achieve success in all areas of your life. Stay committed to your personal growth, and remember that your choices today will shape your future as a leader.

Cultivating a Culture of Responsibility and Accountability on Campus

As aspiring leaders, it is essential to understand the importance of cultivating a culture of responsibility and accountability on campus. In order to achieve success in all aspects of campus life, including effective study habits, time management, leadership, sobriety, morality, healthy relationships, responsible choices, and a serious relationship with God, it is crucial to foster an environment that encourages personal growth and ethical behavior.

One of the first steps in cultivating this culture is to lead by example. As aspiring leaders, you have the unique opportunity to set the tone for responsible and accountable behavior. By consistently demonstrating integrity in your own actions and decisions, you inspire others to do the same. Whether it is being punctual for meetings, following through on commitments, or prioritizing academic responsibilities, your actions will have a ripple effect on those around you.

Another key aspect of creating a culture of responsibility and accountability is promoting open and honest communication. Encourage dialogue among peers, faculty, and staff, to address any concerns or challenges that may arise. By fostering an environment where individuals feel comfortable discussing their experiences, needs, and aspirations, you can better understand the unique dynamics of your campus community and address any issues that may hinder personal growth and success.

Furthermore, it is essential to emphasize the importance of personal responsibility. Encourage aspiring leaders to take ownership of their choices and actions, understanding that each decision they make has consequences. By instilling a sense of personal responsibility, individuals can become more aware of the impact their choices have on themselves, their relationships, and the larger campus community.

Additionally, fostering a culture of responsibility and accountability involves promoting healthy relationships and habits. Encourage aspiring leaders to surround themselves with individuals who share their values and support their growth. By cultivating positive relationships, individuals can establish a strong support system that encourages responsible choices and personal development.

Lastly, emphasize the significance of a serious relationship with God. Encourage aspiring leaders to prioritize their spiritual well-being and seek guidance from their faith. By nurturing their relationship with God, individuals can find solace, strength, and clarity in their decision-making process, leading to responsible choices and ethical behavior.

In conclusion, cultivating a culture of responsibility and accountability on campus is crucial for aspiring leaders seeking success in all aspects of their lives. By leading by example, promoting open communication, emphasizing personal responsibility, fostering healthy relationships, and nurturing a serious relationship with God, individuals can create an environment that supports personal growth, ethical behavior, and responsible choices. Through these efforts, aspiring leaders can navigate campus life with integrity and become resilient leaders in their communities.

Chapter 9: Nurturing a Relationship with God: Spirituality on Campus

Exploring the Role of Spirituality in Leadership

Responsible Choices, Resilient Leaders: Navigating Campus Life with Integrity

In today's fast-paced and competitive world, being a leader on campus requires more than just effective study habits and time management skills. It demands a deep understanding of oneself, a strong sense of purpose, and a connection to something greater than oneself. This is where spirituality comes into play.

Spirituality, often associated with a serious relationship with God, can be a powerful tool for aspiring leaders on their journey towards success. It provides a solid foundation for making responsible choices, cultivating resilience, and fostering healthy relationships – all essential components of effective leadership.

One of the key aspects of spirituality is its ability to guide individuals in uncovering their true purpose and values. When aspiring leaders have a clear understanding of their personal values and beliefs, they can align their actions and decisions with these principles. This alignment not only enhances personal integrity but also inspires trust and respect among peers and followers.

Moreover, a strong spiritual connection can provide a sense of meaning and fulfillment. It helps leaders navigate challenges and setbacks with resilience and maintain a positive outlook. By fostering an inner strength and belief in something beyond themselves, leaders are better equipped to overcome obstacles and inspire others to do the same.

Spirituality also plays a vital role in cultivating healthy relationships. A serious relationship with God encourages individuals to treat others with kindness, compassion, and empathy. It promotes the importance of listening, understanding, and supporting others, which are crucial qualities for effective leadership. When leaders embrace spirituality, they create an environment of trust, collaboration, and inclusivity, fostering a strong sense of community on campus.

(c) 2024: Responsible Choices, Resilient Leaders: Navigating Campus Life with Integrity

Responsible Choices, Resilient Leaders: Navigating Campus Life with Integrity

In addition, spirituality can serve as a moral compass for leaders. It helps individuals distinguish between right and wrong, guiding them to make ethical decisions. By incorporating spirituality into their leadership journey, aspiring leaders can ensure that their actions align with their values and contribute positively to the campus community.

In conclusion, the role of spirituality in leadership is multifaceted and essential for aspiring leaders seeking success on campus. By developing a serious relationship with God, individuals can discover their purpose, make responsible choices, cultivate resilience, build healthy relationships, and lead with integrity. Spirituality provides a strong foundation for personal and professional growth, enabling aspiring leaders to make a lasting and positive impact on their campus and beyond.

Finding Meaning and Purpose in Campus Life

Aspiring leaders on campus often find themselves juggling multiple responsibilities and facing various challenges. It can be overwhelming to balance academics, extracurricular activities, social life, and personal growth. However, by exploring the concepts of finding meaning and purpose, you can navigate campus life with integrity and become a resilient leader.

One of the key elements in finding meaning and purpose is developing effective study habits. As an aspiring leader, you must prioritize your academic success by creating a study routine that works for you. This may involve finding a quiet space to concentrate, utilizing study groups, or seeking academic assistance when needed. By dedicating time and effort to your studies, you not only enhance your knowledge but also set a strong foundation for your future leadership roles.

Responsible Choices, Resilient Leaders: Navigating Campus Life with Integrity

Time management is another crucial aspect of achieving success on campus. As a leader, you must learn to prioritize your commitments and manage your time efficiently. This means setting realistic goals, creating a schedule, and avoiding procrastination. By practicing effective time management skills, you can balance your various responsibilities and make the most of your college experience.

Leadership, sobriety, morality, and healthy relationships are also integral to finding meaning and purpose in campus life. As an aspiring leader, it is essential to cultivate these qualities to create a positive impact on your peers and the campus community. Engaging in ethical decision-making, maintaining sobriety, and building healthy relationships contribute to your personal growth and overall success as a leader.

Moreover, responsible choices play a significant role in finding meaning and purpose. It is crucial to make decisions that align with your values and long-term goals. By making responsible choices, you demonstrate integrity and ethical leadership, setting a positive example for others.

Lastly, a serious relationship with God can provide guidance, strength, and a sense of purpose. Nurturing your spirituality and seeking a deeper connection with a higher power can provide you with the support and resilience needed to overcome challenges and make responsible choices.

(c) 2024: Responsible Choices, Resilient Leaders: Navigating Campus Life with Integrity

Responsible Choices, Resilient Leaders: Navigating Campus Life with Integrity

In conclusion, finding meaning and purpose in campus life is essential for aspiring leaders. By developing effective study habits, practicing time management, cultivating leadership skills, maintaining sobriety, embracing morality, building healthy relationships, making responsible choices, and nurturing a serious relationship with God, you can navigate campus life with integrity and become a resilient leader. Remember, your college experience is an opportunity for personal growth and the foundation for your future leadership roles.

Practicing Mindfulness and Self-Reflection

In the journey of becoming an aspiring leader, it is essential to cultivate mindfulness and self-reflection. Mindfulness, the practice of being fully present and aware of our thoughts, feelings, and actions, allows us to make conscious choices and navigate campus life with integrity. Self-reflection, on the other hand, invites us to examine our values, beliefs, and behaviors, enabling us to grow as individuals and leaders.

In the fast-paced world of campus life, it is easy to get caught up in the whirlwind of tasks, responsibilities, and social interactions. However, by practicing mindfulness, we can bring ourselves back to the present moment and focus on what truly matters. Mindfulness helps us to stay grounded, manage stress effectively, and make responsible choices in line with our values.

One powerful way to practice mindfulness is through meditation. Taking a few minutes each day to sit in stillness and observe our thoughts without judgment can have a profound impact on our mental and emotional well-being. By quieting the mind, we create space for clarity, creativity, and increased self-awareness. This heightened self-awareness allows aspiring leaders to understand their strengths, weaknesses, and areas for growth, leading to personal and professional development.

Responsible Choices, Resilient Leaders: Navigating Campus Life with Integrity

In addition to mindfulness, self-reflection provides us with the opportunity to explore our values, beliefs, and behaviors. It allows us to ask important questions such as: What kind of leader do I aspire to be? How do my actions align with my values? What impact am I having on others? By engaging in regular self-reflection, we can continuously refine our leadership style and make necessary adjustments to ensure we are leading with integrity and authenticity.

Moreover, self-reflection helps us build healthy relationships with others. By understanding ourselves better, we can empathize with and appreciate the perspectives and experiences of those around us. This is crucial for creating a supportive and inclusive campus community where everyone feels valued and heard.

Finally, as aspiring leaders, it is important to remember the significance of a serious relationship with God. Nurturing our spirituality can provide us with a sense of purpose, guidance, and strength. It helps us stay grounded in our values and seek wisdom beyond our own understanding.

In conclusion, practicing mindfulness and self-reflection are essential tools for aspiring leaders. By incorporating these practices into our daily lives, we can navigate campus life with integrity, make responsible choices, build healthy relationships, and cultivate a strong connection with our spirituality. As we embark on this journey of leadership, let us remember to be present, introspective, and faithful, for these qualities will guide us towards success and fulfillment.

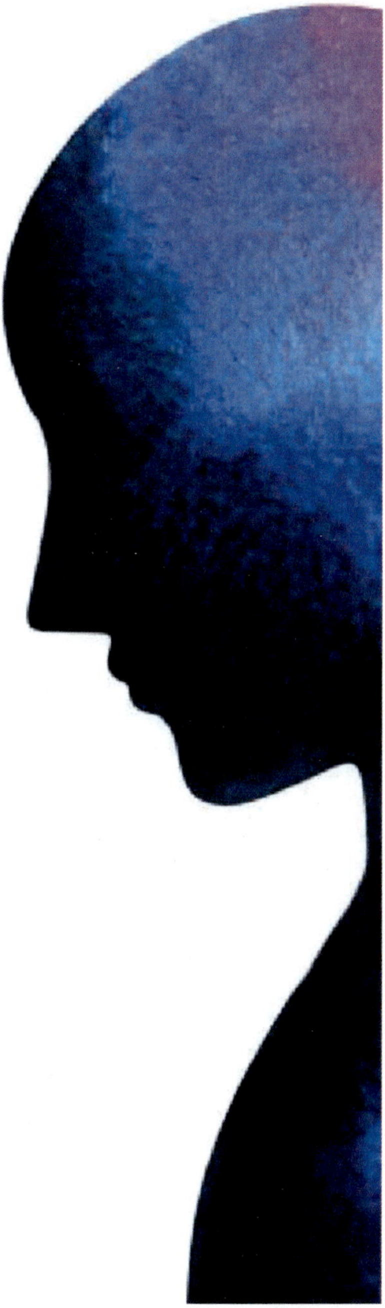

Made in the USA
Columbia, SC
19 March 2024

34026cc8-05ae-4911-8a4d-37abe793d29bR01